go-go dancing for Elvis by Leslie Greentree is the story of two sisters: the beautiful sister, who travels the United States as a dancer for an Elvis impersonator, and her more conventional sister, who stays home and renovates her house. It's a story of love, jealousy, betrayal, and the people who used to have our phone numbers. Most of all it's a story about Hawkeye Pierce and power tools.

D0707541

Also by Leslie Greentree:

guys named Bill

go-go dancing for Elvis
Leslie Greentree

Frontenac House
Calgary, Alberta

Book design by EPIX Design Inc.

The quoted line on page 69 is from If I Were a Bell from GUYS AND DOLLS By Frank Loesser © 1950 (Renewed) FRANK MUSIC CORP. All Rights Reserved

The publisher and author have made all reasonable efforts to obtain permission from owners of previously copyrighted material. In the event that any copyright holder has inadvertently been missed, the publisher will correct future editions.

National Library of Canada Cataloguing in Publication Data

Greentree, Leslie.
  Go-go dancing for Elvis / Leslie Greentree.

  Poems.
  ISBN 0-9732380-2-X

  I. Title.
  PS8563.R43G63 2003   C811'.6   C2003-910035-9
  PR9199.4.G74G63 2003

Frontenac House gratefully acknowledges the support of Canada Council for the Arts and The Alberta Foundation for the Arts for our publishing program.

Canada Council   Conseil des Arts
for the Arts   du Canada

The Alberta Foundation for the Arts   Alberta COMMUNITY DEVELOPMENT
COMMITTED TO THE DEVELOPMENT OF CULTURE AND THE ARTS

Printed and bound in Canada.
Published by Frontenac House Ltd.
1138 Frontenac Avenue S.W.
Calgary, Alberta, T2T 1B6, Canada
Tel: 403-245-2491 Fax: 403-245-2380
editor@frontenachouse.com   www.frontenachouse.com

1 2 3 4 5 6 7 8 9   07 06 05 04 03

for SM

Contents

who we're dancing for

sister from the future

playing house

she was my first kiss   our house was three cozy rooms made
from blankets draping elaborate chair configurations   we'd
take turns being the dad   he had the better role   got to leave
and come back   everything moms did seemed to be some form
of waiting

there was something thrilling about grabbing her from behind
just a little roughly pulling her around to face me   we thought
the harder we pressed our lips together the more meaningful the
kiss   I could feel her teeth against my firmly closed mouth

Mom was just glad we weren't fighting for once   far enough
removed from her own childhood to think her children
innocent   not knowing we drew pictures of naked men and
even more of naked women   clattered our Barbies' plastic legs
together vainly trying to make them fit

sister from the future

she left for Australia a couple of years ago
with five hundred bucks and a backpack
she picked fruit   drove truck   tended bar
did a stint washing paintbrushes for an artist
eventually posing for him while his wife baked gingersnaps
her gift is that the wife didn't mind
couldn't blame her husband for wanting to sketch
the beautiful sister   was a bit in love herself

she called us Christmas Day
I held the phone between ear and shoulder
as I peeled potatoes and checked the turkey
it was Boxing Day in Melbourne
how Star Trek I said
I was laughing until my husband rolled his eyes
and then I stopped
chopped the potatoes with short hard strokes

I thought how fitting it was
to speak to the beautiful sister from the future
I asked her for an inside tip   tomorrow's lottery numbers
thought maybe I would throw these fucking potatoes
in the garbage or better yet just leave them
on the counter to brown and rot
walk out the door jump on a plane
get the hell out of here

go-go dancing for Elvis

why am I always washing dishes when she calls?
she probably thinks I'm one of those people who never
leaves the house   who watches TV all night and thinks
the stars of their favourite shows are real

I sling the tea towel over my shoulder
while she tells me her latest grand adventure
a six month tour across the United States
go-go dancing for an Elvis impersonator
the young slender Elvis of course

she's flying to San Francisco to learn the right Elvis moves
you have to know the right people she says
to be a go-go dancer for Elvis
the beautiful sister has always known the right people
free trips to everywhere   invitations to movie premieres
I guess that means she's always
known all the moves too

what am I supposed to tell her
that I plan to hang out at Totem Lumber in my spare time
next week after I'm finished scraping all the
shit from my walls that was so deftly
hidden by the dainty rose wallpaper put up by the previous
owner   that I was scared to death the first time I
pulled out the lawnmower and how I felt like I'd scaled a
mountain when the grass ended up basically even
and I didn't electrocute myself

while she's being fitted for her black go-go boots
I'll be going through all the boxes I've been avoiding
photographs and wedding shots that never made it into
the album   the birthday cards I didn't have time to
sort before leaving: *happy birthday Honey   thanks for seven
great years   you make me so happy   I love you*

I say I'm fine   ask about the tour   make all those
encouraging envious noises I always make
with the beautiful sister   I hang up the phone and
open a bottle of grenache   I'm not going through
those fucking photographs tomorrow

Anarchy

i.

loose shocks of shaggy brown hair
streak their faces
fall across their open mouths
sweat from blue red yellow lights
trickles down thin tiger striped tees
to leather pants with chains

they were *Anarchy*
or something like that
I can't remember now
but when Kurt sang to me
I was like every eighteen year old girl in the world
dragging myself hand over hand
along the rope that spanned the dance floor
from his groin to my fluttering
unseated dream of glamour

what a joke
I think later
just the poor guy's luck to pick some
virgin who wants to kiss for two hours
who goes home when it's
too late to use that
mass of hair on someone else

ii.

we thought we'd seen the last of them
two months later it's
three a.m. on a Wednesday
when the buzzer rings
Anarchy has a broken van
good thing we have beer in the fridge

you can't maintain sex and sweat
booze and innuendo
for the week it takes to fix their van
we're the envy of our friends
our very own rock band
coming home from hairdressing school to
spaghetti dinners   a fridge full of cold beer
dishes washed   smokes lit
one night we practice fingerwaves in their hair

Kurt and I walk sometimes
past Stuey's ice cream parlour
he tells me about his dog
when we get home he rubs my ticklish feet
I don't pull away
feel myself uncurling secretly toward
his newly gentle hopeless hands
I don't know it at the time
but this will be the only
foot massage I receive for thirty-one years

iii.

Anarchy will be gone tomorrow
van finally taped back together
on their way to a gig in Pincher Creek
the light guy went home on the bus days ago
Kurt wants me to learn to run the lights
try on a whole new life for one week
his hand on my waist is light
it seems so simple

doesn't seem to matter how
tightly I close my eyes
how much I want to
I can't see it
can't imagine myself on the road
with a rock band
what I can imagine:
stale smoke and booze
souring on skin and mouths
expectations and disappointments
missing a week of school
prettier girls

I've never wanted so badly to be
driving toward Pincher Creek, Alberta
in a rusted van
to be the girl who could do that
they drive away
I walk slowly to the fridge but
we're out of beer

girl hopes

mom said it was a sacred moment
the giving up of virginity
would feel good only if I loved him
if I were married
if I brought back the golden apple to
the king at the end of the magic quest
though I wondered exactly how she knew this
her only experience was with the
clumsy farm boy she married

I believed her for nineteen years
held out against a boy who loved me desperately
(cold girl, I grew to scorn his need
shunned him eventually and drank whiskey
for a month to shut out his pleading face)
then past him through the kisses and fumbling
groping fingers of various hungry boys
so dizzy with wanting them fierce inside me
I couldn't walk straight leaving their
mothers' basements at five a.m.

I felt weighted down with it
the only one still lugging this silly stone
knew damn well what I was planning when I
teamed up with the town slut
(she occasionally brought strangers home to
my apartment at four a.m. and
fucked them on the floor –
this is why we eventually stopped speaking
but I've always remembered her claim that
she could come just dancing with someone
and the change that came over her face then –
like a bitch in heat   an embarrassing slack hunger

years later I still miss her broken china laugh
the way she gave smokes to everyone
hugged me hard some mornings)

when I finally shed myself of
my virginity that night it felt like a relief
chose some blandly handsome guy –
damned if I can remember his name now –
of course he didn't call though I
wished he would – I had nothing to say
but there was still that strange girl hope that
somehow this dry tight bony body
had inflamed him to new levels of desire
until he thought of nothing but me
and craved only to have me again
though I didn't crave him at all
kept imagining that sandpaper
feel as he pushed inside
wondered why the build-up was
so much more exciting than the act –

now I wonder at my adamant
refusal to give it up to some two bit
rock star named Kurt – at least he knew
my middle name   laughed in his real voice
we were sober together as much as we were drunk
I don't like to say that I lost my virginity
it wasn't an accident
it didn't fall out of my pocket
I gave it away like a dollar to a bum
didn't feel the remorse I expected, either,
more a blankness   a feeling of my skin
slipping slightly on my bones

borrowed scars

our smaller selves laugh at the camera
she points to the slide
remembers the day she went
down too fast
rolled in panic
head lip tooth striking
rounded metal side
she screamed and screamed
Mom running from
the picnic table
egg salad sandwich falling from her hand
it was the summer we had that
bright blue beach ball
she shows me the scar
pale and hair thin on her lip

I remember the beach ball
too wide to put my arms around
white diamonds on the blue
it was me on the slide
I remember fear
tumbling for hours boneless
rag doll falling silently silently
it wasn't my lip that
finally opened against the metal
but my forehead
just at the hairline
above my eyebrow

this is *my* memory
if not
where did my scar come from

Charlie's Angels

we would race on tiptoe through the house
in Mom's highest pumps
stop   toss our hair
pout our little lips
squeal *freeze*
as we arched our backs and
flexed our calves
trying not to topple from our heels

the blondes were interchangeable
rinsed out and traded in every year or two

Kate Jackson would have been beautiful
if she hadn't been made to stand
beside Jacquelyn Smith all the time

Sabrina was the smartest
the most capable
didn't get herself into foolish messes
always hatched the plan to escape
but her hair didn't flip and curve
in long soft waves

Kelly would put on a Southern accent
at least twice in a season
cajoling truth from the villains
every piece of her
soft and sugar

I knew I should want to be Sabrina
loudly claimed I did
but secretly I wanted to be Kelly

the sorrows of my changing face

> *How many loved your moments of glad grace,*
> *And loved your beauty with love false or true,*
> *But one man loved the pilgrim soul in you,*
> *And loved the sorrows of your changing face;*
>   – William Butler Yeats (*When You Are Old*)

we're sitting at the kitchen table one day
talking about Yeats
drinking cheap white wine from a
carafe that says *cheap white wine*
Kirk my guitar-playing friend is bored and fidgeting
to keep him from drinking our wine
I write out the words to
When You are Old
tell him to go away   put it to music

this is how things happen
a casual comment after a couple glasses of wine
next thing I know three people understand
that all I really desire is for
one man to love my pilgrim soul
at the time I still believe it's possible
from there it snowballs and
one sunny Saturday
he's singing it at my wedding

thirteen years later
I'm watching the wedding video
I got it in the divorce
I'm drinking not-so-cheap red wine
noticing how
from one small moment

that sprang from irritation as much as anything
something lasting was created

I'm also noticing that
even though my lip is curling
and I feel hard and cold as the
diamond that now resides in a safe deposit box
still I love this poem

first trip to Totem

I spent the last hour and a half
peering into the toilet tank
perhaps thinking if I stared at
the part long enough
it would communicate its name to me

his nametag says Darryl
he reminds me of a guy I used to
shoot pool with now and then
wide warm smile
hair flopping on his forehead
the kind of man you don't appreciate
when you're eighteen
now he's someone's husband
Darryl looks like a gentle father
he sets me up with tools, toilet pieces, tips
makes me want to crawl into his lap

pride, however, dictates that I go home
alone to learn to fix a toilet
when it's done
I flush it seven times
surprised each time it works
now I own vice grips

342-ROCK

I flirted shamelessly with the operator while
getting my new phone number
his name was Darryl so I liked him instantly
asked if he was handy with paint brushes
knew the difference between taupe and ecru
when he casually said crap I knew
he was mine   trying to keep me on the line
I was giddy   setting up my new life
but a little talk about paint colours was as far as I took it
as far as I ever take anything

I wish I'd thought to ask for a number
that spells something like *wine* or
free at last free at last thank
God Almighty I am free at last
(but then that would have to be a 1-800 number)
the beautiful sister did of course
her phone number spells *ROCK*
I laughed   applauded her impudence
but secretly I don't think it's that original
I keep wanting to ask her
what she gives the ninth caller

shades of Linda Lee

my phone is haunted by another shadow
her name is Linda Lee
every day there are calls from collection agencies
Linda owes money everywhere and
has skipped town
leaving me with her details
her phone number that doesn't spell anything

I feel a strange sneaking guilt when they call
as if I might really be Linda Lee
they might somehow prove it
the irrational blush of the good girl
accused of lying
who suddenly doubts her own truth

the second week I say things like
Linda's a tour guide in the
Dominican Republic now
I don't think she's coming back
or
Linda left to work with Greenpeace
she disappeared last fall
a tragic dinghy accident   they were
chained to a Russian whaler

these telephone voices remind me of
my ex-husband   parental somehow
slightly disapproving but
too polite to accuse one of anything
to spell it all out

about my hair

something about my smooth hair makes her think I'm repressed
pretending I don't have curls   I straighten it most mornings
say I do my best thinking while blowdrying my hair straight but
when the beautiful sister matches that with the pale lipsticks I
favour it's proof of repression of sexual frustration an old maid a
schoolmarm a woman who hides from life

if she knew what I was hiding if she knew what I do every
Tuesday morning Thursdays between five and seven every
second Friday night and every Sunday morning   if she knew
what I do and how I talk   how my hair falls around and in my
breathless moist lipstick-free mouth   falling tousled and sweaty
across my breasts always tangled
never smooth

The Amazing Elvis And His Next Magical Feat
(for Kimmy)

when I tell him of the beautiful sister's latest plan
he can't quite keep it straight in his head
so many sisters   so many crazy plans
weeks later he's talking with the boys
swapping all those news items from their moms
over frosted mugs   one eye on the game
he tells them he knows a girl who ran away
to become a magician's assistant
she screams with delight when I tell her
what's the difference really
go-go dancer for Elvis or magician's assistant
she'd let any man in sequins saw her in half
in a second if the opportunity arose
she'd get to wear the same
spangled clothes either way

the magician's assistant

we've all seen them
and we've all watched their assistants
silent, always
they are ruby smiling lips and
teased hair
they are barely clothed flesh
in pink spangled spandex

he is the one to garner the applause
we are the ones who cheer as he
throws knives at her
pins her unflinching body to the board
sometimes all he does is change her clothing
from pink to black
she mimes astonishment
but we expected it
we especially like it when he makes her
swallow his long gold sword

we love it when she hands him the tools
to cut her in half
the tools to make her disappear

at the end of the show we applaud them both
his graciousness in clasping her hand
pulling her forward to his side
makes us whistle all the more loudly
when he steps forward for his solo bow

he, after all, is the one with all the tricks
she just stands there
looking pretty
being done to
it is understood that every man in the room
wishes he were a magician

the Spiderman song

the beautiful sister sang in a band when she wasn't painting,
bartending or going to school   I think she sculpted too
occasionally she got a bit part in one of those artsy movies
filmed in Vancouver and seen by two people   I love those
movies especially being the third person to see them

that night her uncombed hair was pulled into two crooked
Minnie Mouse ears high on her head   short tight skirt   black
boots to her knees

she dedicated the next one to me   the Spiderman theme song
with heavy bass and drums I sat at the bar with my vodka tonic
as in love with her as every drunk in the room   the web she
spun was bigger than anything Peter Parker could throw   it
caught us all   not just the thieves

afterward she introduced me to the band   to her friends   her
court   they were so polite to my neat, shining hair and my
tailored pants w. sweater set

last flakes of snow
(for Blaine)

like ashes they drift into my glass of
cabernet   my eyes
watch your tail-lights receding in the night
past the thirty foot
funeral home and crematorium sign
the funeral home flower beds are neatly
overturned   waiting for annuals
there are two young men
I've watched for over a year now
in summer they circumspectly
sweep dust from their sidewalks
solemnly shovel snow in winter
I wonder if each secretly wants to
lob a quick snowball at the
dark suited back of the other
jump in their leaf piles
I can see the back door from my deck
no one steps outside for a smoke
at a crematorium
they never banter   rarely speak
I like their restraint
perhaps these men will treat my
remains with the respect and care
they give their sidewalks

watching Betty

I'm sweeping spider webs from my deck when I see her   huge
and dirt brown marked with white crosses   horns on her back
she is the very queen of spiders   hanging patiently in her
suspended rainbow   I leave the web   it glistens in the
morning sunlight above my front door   I look for her now

Dev and I sit out there one night watching Betty   we have
plastic purple fish glasses filled to the top with crisp sauvignon
blanc and we don't say a word   Betty extricates a fly delicately
from the silver threads and carries it two inches up her web   she
dangles lightly by two legs as she feeds

it's a lazy summer evening and we're slouched in our deck chairs
we brought the ice bucket out so we wouldn't have to move
except to reach for the wine   Mick is a white comma curled
between us nose to toes as we sip in silence
watching Betty

I want to hang upside down in silver be so perfectly myself that
no one could bear to sweep me away

Linda Lee's accountant

strange that a woman who skips out on her bills
would have an accountant
but Linda Lee does
the accountant leaves a message
wanting to confirm tax information
I think *Linda Lee pays taxes?*

when the accountant calls again I tell her the news
Linda came into some money unexpectedly
an elderly man she was kind to on a bus once
he had a bad hip   she gave up her seat
now she's pursuing her dreams
last I heard she was dancing in a Brazilian nightclub
taking voice lessons

the accountant sounds like a nice woman
she has the official voice that comes from spending half
your life on the phone talking about money
we chat for a moment   sigh
wouldn't it be nice to be that free
it's good to know someone's doing it

slumming

it's after midnight when I walk in
I've never set foot in
this dark, smoky hole
but it's a special occasion
and I have my reasons for
all the wine I drank
the faceless men I leaned into
laughing   tonight
reasons for pushing outside my world

doesn't take long for his approach
but the laughing/pretending to enjoy men
portion of the evening is over
everything is rumpled but his lank long hair
now I'm concentrating on serious drinking
shrug him off quick and clean
bat my hand around my head
as if to wave off a fly

he shoots me a grin as he walks away
one that briefly penetrates my
implacable disdain; for a moment
I am rocked by the knowing on his face
rage right back at you bitch

last call; my purse is gone
look around quietly, no fuss
make the late night calls to credit card company, bank
pay the locksmith with borrowed cash
my friends say he came for my purse
they're wrong
I feel that smirk all night
it would cut me to pieces
wait to hear that ineffectual key
scratching at my new brass lock

waiting for Hawkeye

waiting for Hawkeye

she's fucking Elvis
I can tell from her letters
gotta run   Elvis is taking me to
dinner   I'm wearing leopard gloves
with pink maribou trim

I'm waiting for someone
a little less obvious
with less affinity for sequins
a man who prefers a ratty
bathrobe perhaps
like Hawkeye

I would have poured him another gin
had one myself
laughed when he said
champagne's just ginger ale
that knows someone

eight years old and I
knew you Hawkeye
I've been waiting ever since
for eyes that dark
with that much pain
for a man who has dedicated his life to
committing suicide in all
the small ways

black go-go boots

it's stylized sixties   the black boots are to her knees
but the tank top with the silver spaghetti straps and her tiny
skirt only nod to the originals   the colours are
carefully psychedelic

the first photograph shows her and Elvis laughing
her go-go boot draped lightly over his satin thigh
hair pulled high on her head   ponytail cascading over her
shoulders   slapping her in the face as she gyrates

the second is of her in the classic pose   arms pumping
clenched fists   hair flying   boots planted firmly
two feet apart   her head is down   eyes closed
I can feel the music here   something like *Jailhouse Rock* or
his bastardized version of *Hound Dog*

she's having the time of her life
when she wore her boots to supper she felt wild and mod
getting such a kick out of this outfit
like the kid who used to put on the old clothes
from Mom's dress-up box
Elvis told her to go back to the room and change
he's had enough of looking at that crap every night
does he really have to take his work with him to supper?

part of me is glad to see that even a go-go dancer for Elvis
can be made to feel like an idiot   be spoken to in that way
but I still want to drive to their hotel in Reno
and kick his ass

finishing the shiraz

I'm finishing the shiraz staring at the wall when the
beautiful sister calls   drinking from his glass
in a weak moment I tell her and regret it immediately
I thought I wanted to be understood but I don't

she is the only one who knows of him
and she doesn't know much
I thought I wanted to talk about it
tell a few funny stories when I could bear to be flip
but we will only speak of him one more time

perhaps I wanted her to know she's not the only
one having a grand adventure   that I can
be surprising too   there are things about me she
did not know and would not guess
but I have become an entirely different cliché

the other go-go dancer

in every picture she is not quite there
small distances between her
and the others
slightly out of focus
her face cut in half
or clipped rudely at the top
depending on which clumsy tourist
is holding Elvis's camera

she trails softly through my photographs
the other go-go dancer is
pale and slight
sawdust hair in the Austin sun
it's not enough beside the dark
fierce beauty of Elvis or the
crackling electricity of the
beautiful sister

the appeasement of the pregnant woman

they're in Vegas tonight
I know the very room they're playing in
saw Elvis there, in fact
(a different Elvis)
a couple of years ago
the room wasn't as large as I'd thought
and the drinks were about twelve bucks apiece

we'd planned and saved for months
for our girls' weekend
then Darla finds out she's pregnant
joyous news of course
her life's ambition realized
but not on the Vegas weekend
she was so looking forward to the wine
to looking slimmer than the rest of us
in her little black dress

the appeasement begins
Darla wants to see Elvis
Dev and I sneak out for a smoke
ignoring her frowns   her sighs
signaling to the waiter to bring another round
with a club soda for the pouting
plumping beauty in the corner

I don't want to be here
resent the fifty bucks –
it could have bought me
a couple of hours at a blackjack table
laughing with large Americans
checking out their larger diamonds
the drinks would have been free

when Elvis comes on I'm polite
the music is loud   the room small
Elvis is beautiful
slender   heartrending

in the ghetto crashes through us
until even I
the heathen of pop culture
feel the hairs on my arms raise
want to touch that sweaty towel
though not enough
to dive for it
glad now I allowed myself to be
bullied by a sulking pregnant woman

men in jumpsuits

we both favour men in
jumpsuits it seems
although Jean-Luc Picard would
never wear spangles
maintaining his impeccable dignity
even in polyester
Jean-Luc ushered me through
my marriage   seven
years of Earl Grey - *hot*
guided me to honours in a
university Ethics class
he made it clear   neat
never a slut like Riker or Kirk
Jean-Luc was God wandering the universe
but with more consistent rules
more beautiful metaphors

I play the last episode again
yearning for that lost future
watch Jean-Luc finally join the crew
for their weekly poker game
even starship captains have regrets
his final words:
I wish I'd done this sooner

Fargo's, Whyte Avenue

dark ale at your hand
pale at mine
your dark head bent over a poem

three o'clock on a Thursday
I watch the solitary drinkers
the waitress
the way your hair falls over your eyes

you look up to ask
which is more phallic –
to be shot
or stabbed

you think shot
the bullet like sperm penetrating
I say stabbed
the shape of the knife
and how it enters you

we order another round
dry ribs with lemon
I watch your large hands cup the glass
bony knuckles   pared blunt nails
think of your fingers on the inside of my wrist

the sign on the chipped brick wall says
fine food and wet goods

two captains

Captain Jean-Luc Picard   elegant and
imperious   his sharp clean mind
his flute   quoting Shakespeare
even when wakened in the
night his clothes are crisp
I love the resolute little tug he
gives his uniform each time he is
about to take definitive action
I could never live up to Jean-Luc Picard
he would flinch when I said *fuck*
I don't want to touch him
just admire his grace and economy
don't we all crave a man who lives
by the Prime Directive?
it still hurts to watch the episode
where he is captured by the Borg
assimilated   violated with wires
to see that purity damaged

Captain Hawkeye Pearce is always damaged
so perfectly imperfect
I would be the elegant half
until the fourth gin anyway
till we hit the sheets and rolled
around for hours laughing gasping
desperate flawed fucking
I love how his hair is always tousled
falling across his forehead
clothes unkempt stained with sweat
the more blood he is drenched in
the funnier he becomes
the blacker his eyes
he wouldn't let me save him
haunted man   impulsive irreverent

Jean-Luc is an ideal
Hawkeye is a man to hold and heal
lick the salt from his skin
wash his wounds with my tongue

confession in Totem

Darryl and I are almost cheek-to-cheek
leaning over samples in the paint aisle
spinning through sandpapers and primer
I'm thrilled   frightened   breathless
I don't want polyfilla
I want spackle
I enjoy the way my tongue dips and glides
over it: *spackle*
Darryl guides me step by step
lightly steers me to brushes   rollers   trays
spins the roll of green painter tape on his finger
as he waltzes me to the till
when I tell him I love him
he doesn't bat an eye
I wonder how often each day
the men at Totem hear that

by the time she gets to Phoenix

by the time she gets to Phoenix
I'll be working
as she breezes through customs
(security opening her suitcase
just to get a glimpse of
her underwear)
I'll be sitting at the reference desk
looking up number
61 on the periodic table
(prometheum)
or the collective noun
for larks (exultation)
she and Elvis
(and the other go-go dancer
none of us remember her name)
will make their way to the Purple Penguin Hotel
Pool – Sauna – Free XXX Movies!!!
while I think about supper
sit on the floor
brushing the dog
pour my second glass of pinot gris

normal

it was one of those rare days when I hardly thought about you –
I liked it and I didn't – I laughed and had some beer   acted like
a normal girl but I'm not I'm your girl waiting by the phone
knowing you wouldn't call today freed me   I laughed and told
no secrets forgot I had secrets but I had to go home eventually
didn't I and the message light was blinking   one of your non-
messages non-committal   perhaps a hint of relief that I was out
with someone else   I knew my venture into reality was just a
side-trip   an amusement until you returned but you haven't
really returned have you   now the day's laughter sounds shrill
and the beer has just made me thirsty

painting poem

my house is in chaos
furniture lumped in the centre of the living room
draped in old white sheets
plastic everywhere underfoot
kitchen a mass of primer rollers
paint spackle brushes tools
I can't see my table
can't cook a meal wash dishes
have friends over
I don't have the skills to tackle this job
it's no different from thinking I knew
what I was doing when
I got married when I left him
everything in between and since
I can't look at
these rooms any longer or I'll scream
cry beat my fists against these hideous
naked spackled walls but
my bedroom is full of end tables plants
I have nowhere
to go and it's too late to turn back

water over bones

he stands with long arms outstretched on either side holding the
hotel shower rail   weight resting lightly on one naked hip as
water beads over the bones of his ribcage   he watches me with
dark unsmiling eyes as I fall to my knees on the bathmat before
him   lick moisture from behind his knees his calves   when I
take him in my mouth he watches in the large mirror on the far
wall   five naked bulbs surround the mirror drilling into my
damp warm back into the raw pink pads of my feet   my knees
rub thin terrycloth   I feel his eyes on my dark wet head   my
mouth   even as I take him deeper into me I can feel him
slipping away feel myself stumbling in the night

her Elvis lover

I can see it: the dim room
she has sung for him
and she has danced for him
she sees herself reflected in
every taut line of the
body that leans toward her
reaches for her

I can hear her husky voice
tell me how much you want me
what would you do

she feels her skin pearlescent
her eyes dusk and shadow
muscles hum as they
sway toward him
she watches her arms gleam
milky in the dim room
they drape gracefully around him
moonlight plays across her slender flexing calf
it bends fluid on his back
when his tongue touches her
she tastes herself as
musk and loam

say my name
again
again

behind closed eyes she imagines
her own upturned face
dark lashes feather her cheeks
red lips part just so
and *oh*
she is
she

paint, pizza and Linda Lee

I can't find my stove under the paint cans
rollers, trays and remnants of crumpled
dusty sandpaper littering my kitchen
and I'm too exhausted to dig for it
crack a beer to wash the ancient varnish
dust from my mouth   I'm half done by the
time I look up the pizza place
when I say my phone number the kid
at Domino's says *Linda?*
I pause for a second
notice the streaks of brown on the hand
circling my beer can
yeah I say *I'll have the usual*
Linda's pizza will be more exotic
than the pepperoni and mushroom
I was about to order
hang up   finish my beer in three
long gulps before cracking another one
take it to the deck to wait
for whatever Linda has to offer me

Thursday is your garbage day

you had curry last night
sliced tomato
on the side of the plate
played a game of Aggravation
with your kids
read them a story
Thursday is your garbage day

I have seen the paintings on
your walls, just once
the catalogue-tasteful furniture
matches her hair

I know the voices at your office
imagine faces to go with the names
imagine my own voice
is not recognized
I know the grey and silver desk
in the corner office
the cold of its steel against flesh

graffiti

I take the one and a quarter inch angled brush
stir it in the primer
Darryl said it would be good for edging
and I'm sure he'll be right but first

carefully wipe the excess off the brush though
it doesn't matter if I drip
my floor and furniture are covered in plastic
everything but the dog is covered in plastic

stare at my canvas for a while arm poised in air
with my Totem brush and my Totem primer I say it all
dipping and wiping again and again

splash it across my walls in large sweeping letters
stretch out on the couch with Mick draped
sleepy across my knees
cold beer against my forehead watching paint dry

the next morning I cover it neatly with
two coats of swiss charde
but I can feel my words beneath
pushing lightly glowing through the green

once and a half

the first time you undressed me you peeled me like a small cold
girl who had fallen in the snow your hands were gentle and soft
you stroked me like a chickadee who had tumbled from a nest
when I reached out and placed my hand on your ribs slid it up
over the bones I felt your heart race strong and hard felt how
that was for me because of me   I splayed my hand my fingers
on your white skin pressed gently then more firmly until my
handprint was embedded red in your white chest my bones
impressed upon your skin   it didn't fade until after our
breathing slowed   your heartbeat slowed

sometimes I fell asleep with head pressed to your chest   your
long arms wrapped around me once and a half listening to your
heart like a puppy to an alarm clock wrapped in a towel   your
breath echoing those steady true thumps with soft puffs of air
blowing wisps of hair across my cheek in a matching steady beat

how like me to look for symbolism   to ruin the meaning that
did exist   making it more than it was when in a smaller world
it might have been acceptable   trust me to make a metaphor
from a simple physical response

who we're dancing for

spring in Mustang Acres

the chickadees have been with me
all winter   carrying me
through snow with their impudent songs
now daffodils begin to peek through
the thin layers of dust that
drift in from Taylor Drive
coughed up by semis' Jake brakes
through newly opened windows
I hear the neighbour's shrill scream
how many times do I have to
tell you kids

the heavy thud of crows' feet
on my roof is soothing in
their emphatic placement
the rhythmic clacking of skateboards
rings against concrete in the
funeral home parking lot
prepubescent boy throats
cracking open

I lay unsalted peanuts along my
deck rail for the chickadees
watch them scatter and settle
like dandelion fluff
as the blue muscled crow glides in

nine goblets

i.

green and amber
line the counter top
our entire collection
(newly begun last year
hand in hand at out-of-
town garage sales   flea
markets   junk stores)
dried red wine crusts the bottoms
if I did my dishes more often
I would know which glass
your mouth touched last

ii.

I wash dishes around them
watch green and amber glass
for messages   for days
drinking from the bottle
I should know the shape of your mouth
its imprint on glass
on my clavicle
if I wore lipstick at home
I would know which mouth
prints were yours
and which were mine –
but that would be cheating

iii.

on the seventh day I break them
neatly in a velvet bag
tapping them firmly
with a rock hammer
careful not to crush the pieces
take out two shards
one green   one yellow
etch two delicate parallel lines
in the soft inner skin of my right thigh

iv.

hunched over mosaic manuals
from the library armed with tweezers
and magnifying glass
I piece together shards and splinters
fingers sparkling with greengold dust
gently re-break the larger chunks
push them deep in their raw
grout base   embed them
in a gleaming portrait
yellow woman
strangled slowly by green vines

being Bogey

ever since you told me *Casablanca* was your favourite movie
I knew you would leave eventually   could see how the appeal
of sacrificing yourself to a higher good would be stronger than
anything I could offer you   how you were one of those men
who had to do what was right and honourable

you be Bogart then   lay yourself at the altar of an old empty
promise   at the feet of the children who will eventually scorn
your sacrifice as weakness spit I hate you when you won't buy
them a car or this season's green Capri pants whenever they
turn those practised pouting eyes on your stricken face

who shall I be then   Deborah Kerr in *An Affair to Remember*
she too must have always secretly known that love could never
conquer all the pissy details of reality   that's why she couldn't
offer him her flawed self   shall I sit here now with a blanket
over my legs pretending I'm not crippled

the worst part is that even though I've been hit by a truck there
is still a part of me that knows this is the best way to make you
love me   if you had stayed eventually I would have driven you
away in tiny increments with my sharp tongue and my clawing
need

now you will pine for me always and I for you   absence and loss
the only guarantees of a great and lasting love   the ideal and
torment of what's lost somehow more real than making supper
washing dishes taking out the garbage   but I'm still crippled
still sitting under this blanket and I'm not as drawn to the
romance of this movie as you

now he knows my name

I was the one who discovered him in a remainder bin
stayed up late two nights in a row to finish his book
then I dragged myself back to the store after work to
clear out the stock   a copy for every sister and my mom
we talked across B.C. for weeks   in love with
this faceless voice   this seductive goofy Emma-lover
it's my twenty-eight dollar addition to the family mythology

a couple of years later the beautiful sister meets him
at a cocktail party in Montreal
I can't remember now why she was there
but it was some glamorous reason
to do with knowing someone important
I'm sure she was wearing a stunning outfit
that cost her twelve dollars at the thrift store and had
every husband panting after her as she
tossed her hair and made conversation
with their wives

when you're the beautiful sister you can afford
to be generous so she tells him how he made it into
seven women's bookshelves because of me
she knows I will be delighted as she drops my
name repeatedly while plying him with
intelligent praise and insight gleaned and polished
from those long telephone conversations
he is suitably grateful

so am I, naturally, now that he knows my name
it must have been a real toss-up for him between
listening to stories about me   a faceless sister
halfway across the country who shops in remainder
bins or looking at her lovely laughing face

he never wrote another book
she says it's just as well I didn't meet him
he didn't match the voice we loved
she says he's very large
and rather sad-looking

the apples I will add

the day I realize I will die alone the only thing to do is go
shopping   a new blouse won't make a dent in this spasm in my
stomach   I need kitchen utensils   hover over gleaming silver
pots with copper bottoms to match the new knobs for my
cupboards   perhaps cutting boards   a girl can never have too
many   I reject the food processor because it all goes too quickly
slicing by hand turns the preparation of a meal into a three glass
ritual   I stop at the gleaming knives knowing my knuckles will
be bloody for weeks as I get used to them but I've been applying
my own band-aids for years and I am used to slicing myself open
these knives will cut the apples he taught me to add to curry
lemon for the trout I now will eat alone

I unwrap my purchases   pull my glinting new knives from their
box   the instructions flutter to the floor drifting face up across
my foot

never try to grab a falling knife

shopping with Elvis

this week she and Elvis
window-shopped on Rodeo Drive
between shows
no photo this time
I wish there were
how does one go
shopping with Elvis?
does he wear his spangled jumpsuits?
and how does his hair fall
when it's not pomaded back?
does he wink at the clerks   say
how much for the tic tacs?
thank you   thank you very much
when they return to the hotel
does she push his falling hair back
into its pomade?
does he throw his rhinestoned
jacket on a chair
or does she ask him to
leave it on as she
pulls down his fly

ode to a cordless screwdriver

Dev brings her cordless screwdriver
takes me through the three simple
steps of operation for
removing my cupboard doors
it's magnetic   I no longer have to
hold the screws in my
teeth as I juggle
doors hinges screwdriver
this miracle tool was invented by
a divorced woman

my windows are open
Holly Cole is
blasting through the neighbourhood
I'm singing along
cold beer close at hand
the doors come down in fifteen minutes

sanding is next
but first I call Dev
tell her I'm in love with her tool
it was her friend's
but she bought another after six months
when Dev refused to bring it back
I wonder if that will work on her

"if I was a gate"

I thought I loved the cordless screwdriver
but this is something else altogether
I hold my shiny new electric drill
listen to its high-pitched whine
it is fairly leaping in my hand
tingling through my arm my shoulder
waking all my bones

I am a surgeon
drilling tidy holes
precise and perfect
I blow off the dust
step back to admire my handiwork
brandish my shrieking drill
step in again

you have to make small notches first
you see, in the cupboard doors
I could pull out
my old battered hammer
use brute force
I prefer to take the bit in hand
push it gently into the soft wood
make the small circular motions
that create the slot it
will slide into naturally
otherwise it jumps around
eager but awkward
until you guide it home

there is that small moment as the drill bit
pauses   seeks   slips in
a second's resistance before it sinks
I feel the wood yield under my

steady singing pressure
the bit bores deeper and deeper
until with a start I feel it
I am through

now this is power
like when a lover leaves and
your fear turns into the sudden
realization that you can do it for yourself
just as well or better
and you don't have to listen to the same
Monty Python story
over and over and over
throughout the course of a long
beery evening either

Darryl showed me what to do in Totem
it felt heavy and alien in my hands
I wanted to throw myself at his feet
beg him to come home with me
drill my first hole

now I'm laughing aloud
fiercely proud of the naked apertures
racing across my kitchen
like a banner
now I'm looking around my house
wondering what else I can plunge this into

I didn't put music on
wanting nothing to interfere with the
insouciant shrieking seduction of my electric drill
the song fragment that loops through my mind:
if I was a gate I'd be swinging

Linda makes suckers of us all

it's after midnight when I get home
I scratch Mick's belly   let him out
as I retrieve my messages I'm thinking of the man
who asked me out at the wine tasting tonight

there are seven hang-ups

these men will never know how their
casual mention of a coffee next week makes me
want to vomit   I dream that my hair is on fire
wake in the night slapping at my face   lie sweating
I calm myself by planning what to serve next
week with the zinfandels I bought

I am woken at three a.m.   a harsh slurred male voice
slaps me from sleep again   *I know you're there you bitch*
pick up the goddamned phone   Linda I love you

I'm almost tempted to pick up   commiserate
with this drunken fool   lie there instead listening to
the machine   to my heart slamming against my ribs
what did she let them do to her?
and what does she do to them
that they can't forget her?

gift from Baltimore

she remembered my birthday
from Baltimore
my new toolbox is screaming brilliant fire engine red
rectangular and solid with silver hasps
a lid that clangs lightly
I close it   open it again
inside: a removable tray for nails and screws

below lies the perfect hammer
the head shines   the glowing wooden handle
curves to nestle perfectly in my open palm
hard and warm as my fingers curl around its
heavy satin   leading my arm in
long flowing strokes through the air
my red toolbox sits at my feet
hammer at rest now at my side

the photo is dated: 9:47 a.m. November 13 –
on the back: *can't wait to come home and*
see your drill holes
give my love to Mick
she is wearing flannel pyjamas
similar to mine
she looks tired
I begin to plan her welcome home

New Orleans

for the first part of Carnival
she sends photographs
glowing from them in her
gold Carnival Ball mask
iridescent plumes floating
above her head
purple feather boa tossed naturally
around her slim shoulders

in the next shot they are on the street
she brighter than Elvis again today
neck draped in beads of
green gold and purple
the official colours of Carnival
she explains
green for faith
gold for power
purple for justice

I know what girls do
to earn their beads
imagine the shouts of drunks
leaning from windows on Bourbon Street
the crowd one laughing drinking organism
calling *show us your tits*
of course she would
it's all part of the fun
no one cares what her tits look like
it's the act itself that earns
approbation and gifts of beads

(although the breasts of
the beautiful sister are
spectacular anyway
of course)

there at Carnival I, too
might allow myself to be
carried away finally
flash my breasts
at strangers for baubles

my breasts and I

I didn't like to be on top because my breasts swung wildly   it's
just too hard to come when you're thinking about whether or
not your breasts are longer than his penis and I don't think most
women need one more reason to feel badly about their bodies,
or one more distraction that diverts them from the goal   the
upshot of the matter is that I preferred the missionary position
for reasons that had nothing to do with prudery and everything
to do with television

I run my hands over my breasts down to ribs and hipbones
trying to remember how it was to feel beautiful   to drop my
clothing slowly to the floor straighten and turn with certainty to
an admiring gaze

I hated them until he was kind to them but what does that
matter since my breasts and I are alone again   they may not be
perfect when seen up close but they have done well for me in
sweaters for years now   catching me looks and whistles from
idiots who still somehow make me feel good as long as they
never get close enough to discover the truth

who we're dancing for
(for Joan)

my freshly painted home
seafood curry with
cherry tomatoes and cucumber
pears with brie for dessert
Oregon pinot noir
I'm opening the second bottle
alone but not really
the beautiful sister is here as usual
hovering brave and bold and gorgeous
in the air above my dirty dishes
fuck you   I tell her
swirling rubies in my glass   my mouth
breathing in the long finish
don't you know we're all
go-go dancing for Elvis?

making way

night time   eyes closed
turning my bed around in my mind
making the room spin slowly until finally
when I opened my eyes
my skin crawled and leapt with shock
to see the wall where the open room should be
sometimes I steered my bed to the top
of the stairs   or into my sister's room
I don't remember doing it after leaving Lamming Mills

the last time I recall seeing air
was in Dawson Creek   I must have been about
nine or ten because this memory takes place
in that old army house with the huge dining room
if I fuzzed my eyes a little   unfocused them
there it was   shimmering
I could turn my head slowly   see air
everywhere   almost hear the
molecules vibrating suspended before me
just a view I'd slide into by accident sometimes
it took years to notice it was gone

flying was the last to go
it happened only once in high school
I couldn't soar as high as usual but I only
kicked lazily   not really noticing
not knowing it would be my last flight
it was a dark night and I was happy to be flying again
hovering a couple of feet above the telephone wires in
Coleman   fearless joyful   looking for landmarks
I went right over Darryl Zak's house and Chris's Café
before swooping home to be grounded

flying is what I have always missed the most
but the other day I suddenly remembered
I can no longer invert the universe either
and air is now invisible to me

green, gold and purple

green for faith
my living room   a new ocean of green
swiss charde walls   one deep pine
blinds half closed so the plants
swim through the sunbeams
bright ivy   misty Chinese evergreen
nestled against the arbor couch
the dusty ficus bought for the name
more than the colour
fifteen dollars on sale
an emerald formica-topped thrift store desk –
bought the same day as the ficus
with five bucks left for the rest of the week
if green is for faith
I must have some after all

gold for power
bright marigold slashes on my cushions
court jester triangles of it hang above windows
a small lemon lamp on the table
(my husband and I spoke quietly   viciously
to each other as I chose it
clutching the box saying
I'd never experienced anything so
painful as the purchase of a twenty dollar
yellow lamp while he stared at the wall and
pretended not to hear)
a gold candle here   a yellow plant pot
there   and in the wine rack, of course
several bottles of Yellow Label
there's power in taking the lamp that made
me admit, finally, that my marriage was over
that and a full wine rack

purple for justice
the shade I chose for my bedroom
wild turkey
but it doesn't have the same dignity
this particular shade is all mine
the guy in the paint store was politely dubious
and I thought to myself
that's why I'm not asking anyone's opinion
mornings it's mauve but by two-thirty
in the afternoon mid-summer it's
bright enough to make you blink fast
it softens at dusk to wild heathery shades
I like that I don't know
what I'm getting different times of day
it seems as real a form of justice as one can hope for

moving through my little house
Tom Waits on the CD player   I hit it
right the first time: *new coat of paint*
pull my shirt over my head
throw it on the floor   finger-comb
my tangled hair   arch my back
reach behind   unhook my bra
toss it over the small lemon lamp
dance through my house
past the open window shades
the dog gamely joins me   dashes through
the room   barks along with Tom
I offer a deep bow to the gallery outside
head flung back   arms outstretched
Mick panting at my feet

she wears her faith, her power and justice
tossed around her neck
I cover the walls and the furniture with mine

kitchen wall

it's called wild rice
once two coats are applied
it is the colour of
melted chocolate ice cream
the creamy chocolate pink it becomes
after you've gently swirled it
with your spoon around and
around the bowl
smoothing and blending and warming
watching it drip from the spoon
in thick rich clumps
glorious eons of anticipation
one of the few times I didn't even register
my mother's impatient sigh
now I lean forward
lick my kitchen wall

imagining Linda Lee

Linda Lee
it sounds like the name of a porn star
nearing forty
pretty in a hard bottle blonde sort of way
the kind of woman dumb saps
drink themselves into a stupor over
punch out windows for

she's the neighbour who mows the lawn in a bikini
the old man next door staring openly until
his wife shoots him that disapproving look
and he tears himself away from the sight of
her thin, slightly mottled thighs

she's a woman who keeps her options open
splits when she doesn't like what's happening
she leaves behind the people like me
who dutifully return calls
stay where we're supposed to
surprise no one

poorman's jambalaya

white pepper black and cayenne
measure carefully then add another shake or two of each
hot peppers are mildly addictive

crumble cumin add thyme dry mustard grainy
chunks of sea salt to a yellow bowl
four bay leaves and sift gently

drizzle over sparking ham green pepper smoked sausage
onions and celery   the spices will crust all they touch
browning and crisping the greens and whites
curling through your wakening mouth your nose

these aromas will linger in your kitchen for days
seep again from your frying pan
each time you soap and rinse it

add stock with fresh parsley rice and simmer
wait with watering mouth
discard bay leaves   scoop steaming heaps on
warmed plates with stars of crudités

open your mouth to a spoon spilling jambalaya
your faithful mind will feel the heat as pain
reward your offering of peppers with a gentle creeping
euphoria   flooding you with a natural morphine
it will expand from mouth to mind to shoulders spreading
throughout your pleased stunned body
its offering a natural response to perceived danger

Chef Paul Prudhomme says each pepper offers its own
seductions to the palate at different moments –
the first forkful in your mouth will burst and startle

to be followed by a deep and mellow fire as you chew
pinpoints of pleasure localized on every part of your tongue
swallow reluctantly the next forkful
already poised to your lips

the art of pepper gestalt is a fine one
Paul sautés his vegetables for varied lengths
of time   adding texture and crunch to the dish
when balanced correctly against the perfect blend of peppers
your mouth will shimmer for hours with what he calls
the "after-you-swallow" glow

Acknowledgements

My heartfelt thanks to Blaine Newton, Kimmy Beach, Pat Horner, Joan Crate and Rae Anne Greentree for your excellent comments and insights. You have all helped to make this a much better book. Thanks to each of you, too, for the remarkable friendships and the wine we have enjoyed while making this a better book, and for your generosity in sharing your own considerable talents with me.

A special thank you to Rian for helping me to come up with the title (over wine, naturally) before a single poem had been written. More thanks to my Thursday night group: Joyce Middlestead, Bruce Strand, Judy Larmour and Pam Yule-Charles for their help in workshopping many of these poems.

My gratitude, as usual, to my family: Rae Anne, Gerry, Mike, Rian, Dev, Warren, Sheila, Tyler, Terry, Elise, Dominique, Sam, Shea and Mick, for your love and encouragement. Thanks to my wonderful friends and colleagues at Red Deer Public Library and Red Deer College, as well.

Leslie Greentree was born in Grande Prairie, Alberta, and has
lived in various parts of BC and Alberta, including Salmon
Arm, McBride, Dawson Creek, The Crowsnest Pass, Calgary
and Lethbridge. She works at the Red Deer Public Library as the
Marketing Assistant and as an Information Services Assistant,
which means her mind is filled with useless bits of trivia she
pulls out as her only party trick. Her first book, guys named Bill,
was published by Frontenac House as part of their poetry series
Quartet 2002.

guys named Bill

*Greentree's narrator holds your attention the same way that an
acquaintance at a party does -- not because of how she speaks, or
even what she says, but by the sheer force of inwardness mutating
into revelation.*
  – Alexander Rettie, *Alberta Views*

*The various characters named Bill become a recurrent thread or droll
motif that runs throughout the book; they appear like so many anti-
Kens or Prince Charmings at meaningful moments in the narrator's
life, and represent various way stations along a path of emotional and
spiritual growth.*
  – Richard Stevenson, *Lethbridge Insider*

Cheeky, sexy, and pulls no punches.
  – Kimmy Beach, *The Electric Ant*